Penny Stocks Investing For Beginners:

Penny Stock Trading Guide

By

Robert Alderman

ISBN-13: 978-1503273771

Table of Contents

Introduction 5

Chapter 1. Penny Stock Basics 7

Chapter 2. How to Invest in Penny Stocks 9

Chapter 3. How to Find The Best Penny Stock? 11

Chapter 4. About Stock Brokers 15

Chapter 5. How to Start Investing in Penny Stocks 17

Chapter 6. 6 Effective Strategies for Penny Stock Starters 19

Chapter 7. Trading Methods to Know 25

Chapter 8. 5 Top Trading Tips and Tricks 27

Final Words 30

Thank You Page 31

Penny Stocks Investing For Beginners: Penny Stock Trading Guide

By Robert Alderman

© Copyright 2014 Robert Alderman

Reproduction or translation of any part of this work beyond that permitted by section 107 or 108 of the 1976 United States Copyright Act without permission of the copyright owner is unlawful. Requests for permission or further information should be addressed to the author.

This publication is designed to provide accurate and authoritative information in regard to the subject matter covered. This work is sold with the understanding that the publisher is not engaged in rendering legal, accounting, or other professional services. If legal advice or other expert assistance is required, the services of a competent professional person should be sought.

First Published, 2014

Printed in the United States of America

Introduction

The common notion of investment in stock is that's its speculative. This mindset has created a lot of fear among the investors and the ones who tries to step in stock business. The improper knowledge and misleading guidance has deviated the people's mind and distracted them from the path of the business. Whereas, the need of investment in business has raised in the current era, as the boundaries of investors are getting wider and wider.

At many times the opportunities are knocking at the door but our fears does not let them in. This has created a great void between what we wish and what we actually do. Life cannot be led by fears, the only way to make your dream comes true is to own them and pursue them. Otherwise, the business opportunities will come in and left without bringing any improvement in your current state.

The decision to invest in stock is always hard, knowing it involves the great risk. However, the proper guidance and knowledge of any business can make you a successful investor and gainer. It all can only be possible by following the proper strategies and investing at the right time.

Timing does matter in every field of life whether its exam, job interview or to make any decision. The things done at the right time can bring fruitful results. Learn how to use the best strategy at the right time to start investment and earning through stock market. This step by step guide will help you to master the field and to setup your new successful business within short duration.

Chapter 1. Penny Stock Basics

In stock business, the penny stock is also known as micro-cap stocks. Previously, it is famous for investing under $1, but the current terms has changed penny stock investments as under $5. Although currently, the trading is made above $1 even then it's called penny stock due to previously perceived terms. It is known as one of the high risk stock trading, but some wise strategies can be helpful to save you from any risk. However, as you are investing little money the trading might be of high risk but the chances of losing bigger amount is too trivial here.

How actually the Penny stock investing works?

The famous saying is "A penny saved is a penny earned. However, it is not almost right and especially for the penny stock investing. Here the story could be different, if the penny invest sometimes result in penny lost. Penny stock is based on trading money under $5. Penny stock works differently than the regular stock business advertising their bid prices or regular bidding in newspaper, TV and other media resources. Whereas, in penny stock the broker or agent is involved to arrange the trade for you by bid on the price, someone willing to buy or sell the stock.

Most commonly penny stock involved the new startups who are looking for quick break through and the investors who are looking for some quick bucks. The difference between the selling and buying bid determine, how much money you will lose or gain. The penny stock trading is controlled by brokers and sometimes they manipulate the bids for their own personal gain. Choosing the right broker is the key to get the success in the stock market.

Chapter 2. How to Invest in Penny Stocks

Step No. 1: Finding The Right Broker

First thing is to find the right broker with the less fee charges and high execution rate. If you will be paying high fee, it will cost you more than you gain. The broker must be responsive, quick and smart. The slow trading execution will earn you money losses as the stock market trends fluctuate quite frequently. If you are not keeping up to them, it would be possible that the market trends may take an opposite direction and you will lose a lot of money. So keeping up with the market trends is important to really gain profit from the investments.

Step No. 2: Find The Right Companies to Invest

Next important thing is to find the best companies and potential businesses to invest your money through penny stock. The random invest can sometimes make your luck works but it's not always true. So finding the right company for money investment requires an in-depth analysis and market research. Keep a good eye on the current market trends and invest in the companies accordingly. You have to learn the strategies by experiencing yourself, so always try to learn from your failures to avoid any misfortune in the future.

Step No. 3: Be Active and Dedicated

Penny stock investing requires constant commitment and frequent checks on the market trends and investments. Trading in stock is not something about holding and wait, it needs constant research, planning and decision making. The trading even take place multiple times in a day, so for investment and being a successful penny investor you need to dedicate an ample amount of time and have to stay active throughout the day to gain some handsome amount of profit.

Chapter 3. How to Find The Best Penny Stock?

Finding the right penny stock for trading is the most crucial and daunting thing. The penny stocks are small investments has not much words about the success or loses are whirling around. Even you won't get any good information on which one is the best or which one is scam. With lack of knowledge and experience it becomes very risky to go for any penny stock and invest your money into it. Amidst of all this confusion and risk, it is quite tricky to find the best penny stock to gain safe profit. These simple tips will help you find the right penny stock:

1. Subscribe the free newsletter of penny stocks

Find the penny stock traders are subscribe their free newsletter by using your email. Once you have subscribed to enough number of penny stock, you will start receiving their updates, deals, news in your email. Always read the disclaimer at the bottom of the email to know why company is advertising and what is the motivation behind it? It is very important to understand the intent of the newsletter.

Be cautious, because they have various criteria and some are paying the shares to pump up their prices only. Do not go for those penny stocks, charging extra money, taxes and any other form of fees. Be aware of scams out there.

2. Paid Penny Stocks

Some of the penny stocks offered paid services to get access to their newsletter and important content. It is not bad to pay for the services which are authentic and of good reputation. Attain the membership and stay updated with the latest market trends and tricks to make more using penny stock. They even covered feature penny stock traders and you can get good idea of other penny stock traders out in the market. Understand the motivation behind the penny stock traders. Always analyze the facts critically to make a wise decision without falling into any manipulation made by the penny stock traders. You hard earned money is involved, so don't take things easy.

3. Find and study the experts of penny stock market

Whenever we start anything, we always look for inspirations to keep ourselves motivated on the path and make more out of it. The penny stock market also has its own experts, reading through their lives you can get a lot of inspiration and tips to kick start your business in penny stock trading.

You can easily find the inspiration stories of the experts, mostly the market gurus are well known and easily found on the web. Join their newsletter, keep yourself up to date by reading their articles, books and strategies. You will get a lot of people there too, through their comments and taking part with discussions. The right strategies to get success in the market could be discovered.

Look for the penny stock traders and brokers too, these experts are trading with. Join those brokers are start making money. Do regularly check their updates on the site and in your email to learn the latest market trends and techniques capable enough to turn market into your favor.

4. Learn the tactics and techniques

Penny stock trading will open the new doors of learning on you. Whether you are reading your newsletter, analyzing the market or investing money in the market by finding the best broker. You constantly learning the ways to do something better. Always learn from your mistake and try not to repeat them.

You can read many tricks and techniques everywhere, but you can't get good hands on them until or unless you really imply them practically by keeping them in mind while investing money in penny stock. The things you experience yourself last longer than the things you just listen and see. So experience the guru within you by taking the charge of your success and failure.

Chapter 4. About Stock Brokers

When you enter the stock market, the encounter with the specific term is quite frequent. It is necessary to understand the market terms and their usage. Similarly, when you start searching for the right penny stock or brokers, you need to know what actually brokers are. What they are capable to do and how many types of brokers in the market? Without knowing this all, you can't get to the place where you really want to reach.

First thing you must know about is stock brokers and start your search for the best stock broker. The stock brokers are the agents or the company which conduct the selling and buying of your shares within the stock market. There are two types of stock brokers exist in the market the full service stock brokers and the discount stock brokers.

1. Discount Stock Brokers

The discount brokers are offered the few services like recommendations, suggesting the portfolio and answering the queries. The trade on very low commission rate and in return it is quite beneficial in terms of the investor. You can get both offline and online discount stock brokers. However, the online discount broker is best, as you can check their trades and other details from anywhere and stay up to date about the market and about your account.

2. Full Service Stock Brokers

The full service brokers also give you advice, suggestions and recommendation, but their services are paid. To attain their services, you need to pay high fees and it is suitable for only those investors having a big amount of money to invest. Although they provide the quality services and you earn a lot of profit, but your most of the profit will spent in paying their high fees.

Chapter 5. How to Start Investing in Penny Stocks

To take a start in the penny stock investing, you need to do the extensive market research. Understand the terms and find the right broker. Once you have enlisted the best brokers, choose the one offering free services or having less fee, plus offering an online account. Set an online account with the stock broker, as you need to sign in the account multiple times within a day.

The second thing is to be realistic, understand the risk involve in the penny stock investments. Because the penny stock trading involves either the new startup companies or the ones at the edge of bankruptcy. These small companies are mostly not enlisted on the famous or established stock exchanges and mostly are not adhere with any signed closure, so the money you are investing is quite risky. You will also need to remain be aware of the scam brokers and companies.

Keep your research skills on. Constantly look for information about best practices to follow while investing in penny stock. Follow the guru of the stock market and stay updated with the latest trends and techniques commonly practice in the trading market. Attend the events online and companies involved in the penny stock trading. Research on your own and do not rely solely on the information provided by others.

The continuous research is the key to success. Do not trust blindly any broker, ask questions, and stay up to date with the latest terms of the market. If you are investing your money, it is necessary to protect it by making more profit. Penny stock investing demands the constant check and balance, though you are investing less amount of money, but penny stock is nothing about spend and stay calm. Login into your account 3 – 4 times a day and check the market condition frequently.

Chapter 6. 6 Effective Strategies for Penny Stock Starters

Trading in penny stock has become popular during the last decade, as thousands of investor has earned a huge amount of money within the short duration. Penny stock trading is famous for investing low and earning big in little time as compared to regular stock exchanges and trading. The speculators can take benefit by earning huge amount of money by putting less amount on risk. Investing in penny stock is best for the beginners and those owing low amount of money.

As getting success in any business depends on the strategies adopted, the penny stock investing is also dependent upon the strategies you adopt to get success. The penny stock gurus out there are suggesting many strategies to get success in the penny stock business and some of the most effective strategies are as follows:

1. Continuous monitoring of the stock trends

As mentioned before, the best way to get more money out of your investment is to keep a good eye over the fluctuations happening in the stock market by continuously updating yourself with the market trends. Penny stock fluctuates too frequently and by taking benefit of any instant you can make a bigger sum. Many studies have confirmed that the short term investment strategies are the best to gain more profit than investing in long term shifts, where one fluctuation could cause you a huge loss of money. So, take advantage of the momentary changes in the stock market and earn the profit successfully.

2. Avoid the Hype

As the penny stock is getting famous among investors and people looking for some quick bucks, some companies have started to increase their stock value for little duration to encourage the inexperienced and new investors to purchase their stock shares in large amount. As a result the company sell their shares on high amount to another company and earn a lot of profit.

It is necessary to research and analyze the previous track record of the company. Sudden fluctuations can be false and must be avoided to invest in those companies which shown a sudden change in their stock value. It is important to know, which one is the good investment company and which is not, sometimes falling in false trap the beginners lost their all amount.

3. Use of Famous and effective Strategies

The other factor which is crucial in deciding the fate of your money is how effectively you are using strategies learned and how effectively you can predict the company stock value. The best strategy is to consistently trade with the one company and spend enough time to know the company record and previous stock value. Sticking to one company for a while can also earn you a lot of benefits.

Penny stock investing is not always like gambling, even though you could not be 100% sure of the profit but you can predict the next bid by keeping in mind the history fluctuations of the same company. Do keep in mind that the most of the companies associated with the penny stock market are those who generate low amount of profit each month. These low earning companies are more prone to collapses in the market than the companies, constantly earning substantial amount of profit each month.

Always choose those companies who are keeping themselves with the current trends of product purchases and developing product and services in demand. Secondly, look for their customer's range, the best strategy is to go for the one having diverse geographical customers.

4. A good analysis of the shares Volume

The fourth important strategy is to go for those companies, having a good volume of shares running in stock market. In day trading, the investors can purchase a huge volume of the shares of the same company in very low price and if the values of the stock go up within the same day, the profit earn will definitely be huge.

The other important thing is to research the market and look for the potential investors interested in purchasing the same company's shares. If the company's share is in demand, then on opening of the market the shares get sold too quickly and converted into the profit instantly. Using this effective strategy, the risk of loss can be avoided and you can play your game in the safe zone. So always analyze the market to pick the best companies having huge volume of share in the penny stock.

5. Take advantage from the Volatility

Trading with the famous and well known stock traders, mostly companies have to hold their stocks for years before they can sell for making profit. In this time period, the companies sell their assets and get acquired by other companies. The penny stock market is more volatile than the other traders and you should go for the companies whose stock values fluctuate frequently during the one day of trading.

This strategy is little bit risky than the others one, but it will ensure that the company is not holding the share for the longer period of time and constantly selling and buying. You do not have to wait for long to have some profit. This strategy is known as the best one for earning some short term profits irrespective of the high risk involved.

6. Timing Does Matter

In penny stock investing, when the share value of the company drops, the investors try to liquidate the shares at very low price. This is the best time to large volume of the shares at very low price. Once you acquired the stock at low price, keep a good eye on the stock fluctuations until it reaches at the highest price.

Once the stock value is at its maximum, sell the shares and earn a substantial amount of profit. It may take some days or time to reach to the maximum value but at the end you will earn your handsome amount of profit. But do not forget to analyze the track record the company before investing into low stock value.

Chapter 7. Trading Methods to Know

To start with the penny stock investing, a lot of thoughts are required towards the methods and strategies to be adopted for becoming a successful trader. Penny stock is risky and not suitable for the ones having fear of taking risk in the business. The frequent fluctuations in the stock values during the day can earn you both loses and profits. The things move faster in penny stock trading than in any other trading exchange. There are two methods by following which you can even easily earn a big profit while playing at risk.

1. Buy and Sell Method

The first method is bur and sell. You buy the shares of the company at the low price and sell it at the highest profit. It will simply make you earn some good amount of profit straight forwardly. For example you buy the shares at $1 and sell them at $1.25, it simply earn you 25% profit within a day. However, this method is totally dependent on the stock price to go up, if it would not go up then it could cause you more loss than benefit, but it all depends on the company reputation you are trading with.

2. Buy Back Method

The second method is quite tricky. You borrow the shares from the broker at the current price, and when the company shares go down, you buy the shares from the company at the low price and return the same shares to the broker. If the stock was at $1.25 while you borrowed it then on returning it to broker at $1, you will earn 25% profit. However, it could turn both ways, like if the stock goes up, you will end up losing the more money than you had invested.

Chapter 8. 5 Top Trading Tips and Tricks

Here are top tips and tricks to successfully trade in penny stock market:

1. Ignore the fake penny stock stories whirling on the social media and on the internet freely. Not all the success stories you found on the net are authentic, so stop focusing on reading the success of others and work on searching new strategies and techniques to earn some solid and long term profit, instead of playing for your luck.

2. Always read the disclaimer: While searching for some good penny stock websites and newsletter, do not subscribe to each and every newsletter, as it will cost you more time while figuring out what to read in your inbox and what to not. Therefore, always choose wisely, by first going through the disclaimer of the website. Find the associations of the website and if it is authentic and well known penny stock providers, only then subscribe them.

3. Do not hold the shares for long: The best thing you can do to earn quick profit is to sell your shares quickly. As the share price hit the maximum value, sell the share quickly.

Sometimes people shoe greediness and think that by holding on to shares for some more days will earn them more profit and that the company shares will go up more in next couple of days. Unfortunately, it does not happen and cause more loses than benefits.

4. Do not trade large portion and positions: Be careful never trade at large positions. Secondly, do not invest all of your money in buying the large size shares of the same company. No doubt if the value goes up, you will easily earn more but think if it goes down the loss will be equally shocking. So avoid to take risk in investing in just one company's stock.

5. Do not let yourself get trap in the lock of stock: The stories in the newsletters are quite manipulative and it is quite hard to keep yourself unbiased. So, be cynical and do your own research and analyze the market carefully. Ask the people already trading in the market and go for the real people and listen to their stories and tips. Instead of following the stories published online, they may be fake and can put our money at risk.

These simple tips can save you from huge loss in the stock market. Mostly, people stepping in the business do not know from where to get the information and how to authenticate, this miserable situation lead them to be trapped by the scammers and fraudulent out there waiting for their new victims.

Final Words

Nothing in the life is easy and trading is for sure not the one of easiest thing to do. Especially, it is not for those people who cannot afford any risk in their lives. A person who is free from fear can only remain consistent in the stock trading investing, otherwise many people come and many go away. The effective strategies and tricks can't be learn in days, it takes months or years to be a money making guru in the field of stock trading.

The famous traders have earned their place in the stock market by continuously striving for the best practices to adopt and implement. If you want the ultimate success in the penny stock investing and want to become the next penny stock guru than follow the guidance provided above and one day you will surely stand the success, which is store only for the lucky ones.

Thank You Page

I want to personally thank you for reading my book. I hope you found information in this book useful and I would be very grateful if you could leave your honest review about this book. I certainly want to thank you in advance for doing this.

www.ingramcontent.com/pod-product-compliance
Lightning Source LLC
Chambersburg PA
CBHW070732180526
45167CB00004B/1722